What Do You Do
When You're Scared
of The Dark?

What do you do when you're scared
of the dark?

Do you put blankets on your head?

Do you jump at every bump and bark?

Or hide under your bed?

When all the light that you can see is
coming from the moon,

Do you feel like dark is covering you?
And every part of your room?

Do you pretend to be an astronaut?
Flying into space?

Or maybe that you're fighting
crime, with a smile upon your face?

When you're in bed, sometimes it's hard to quickly fall to sleep.

Do you think about what you did today? Or maybe you count sheep?

Do you dream of what you want to do and what tomorrow brings?

Or do you lie awake at night listening to yourself sing?

When you are scared of what's around, and what you cannot see.

Remember dark is simply that the sun has gone to sleep.

The moon is out and shining, and bright enough for night.

So, try to get some sleep my love with just this little light.

You're not alone in thinking, that dark is here to scare.

But dark is fine, and you're alright so squeeze your teddy bear.

You're loved and safe and oh so sweet, so close your little eyes.

Tomorrow comes so quickly, to which is no surprise.

Sweet dreams my little darling,
there's nothing left to fear.

I'll see you in the morning, and
I am always here.

Have you seen Sam The Luckiest Clover?

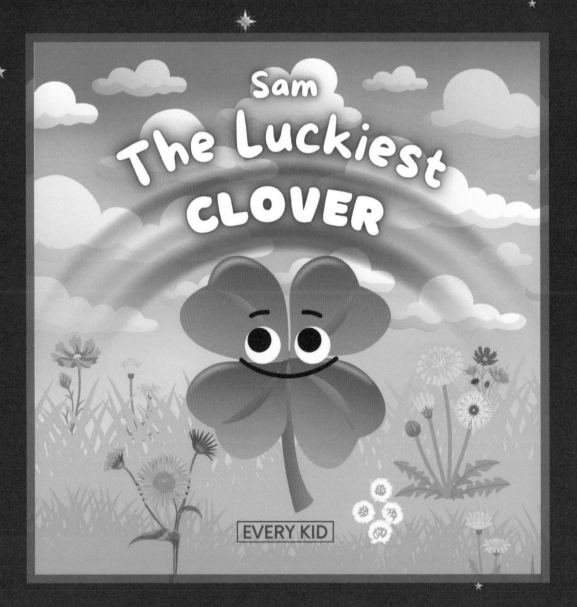

Check Out Our Other Books!

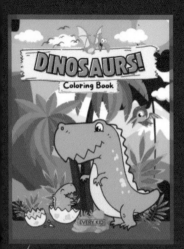

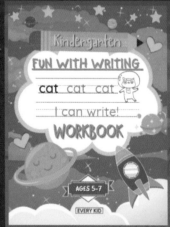

EVERY KID

Foster The Magic
Within Every Kid

Printed in Great Britain
by Amazon

81244966R00018